CRETE

IN SEARCH OF ANCIENT CRETE

Piero Ventura and Gian Paolo Ceserani

Silver Burdett Company

Morristown, New Jersey

In Search of Ancient Crete
Copyright © 1985 Arnoldo Mondadori Editore S.p.A., Milan
Translated from the Italian by Michael Shaw
Editor Philip Steele
Design Sally Boothroyd

First published in Great Britain in 1985 by
Macdonald & Co. (Publishers) Ltd.
London & Sydney

Adapted and published in the United States in 1985 by
Silver Burdett Company, Morristown, New Jersey.

All rights reserved

Printed and bound in Spain by Artes Graficas Toledo S.A.
D. L. TO: 1106 -1985

Library of Congress Cataloging in Publication Data
Ventura, Piero
  In search of Ancient Crete.

  Summary: Describes the archaeological excavations on the island of Crete that revealed the remains of the legendary Minoan civilization which flourished from about 3000 to 1450 BC when it was destroyed by the effects of a volcanic eruption.
  1. Minoans – Juvenile literature. 2. Crete – Antiquities – Juvenile literature. 3. Knossos (Ancient city) – Juvenile literature. 4. Evans, Arthur, Sir, 1851-1941 – Juvenile literature. 5. Greece – Antiquities – Juvenile literature. [1. Minoans. 2. Crete – Antiquities. 3. Knossos (Ancient city) 4. Evans, Arthur, Sir, 1851-1941. 5. Archaeological expeditions] I. Ceserani, Gian Paolo, 1939- . II. Title.
DF220.V38   1985   939'.18   85-40414
ISBN 0-382-09120-5 (soft)
ISBN 0-382-09117-5 (lib. bdg.)

Contents

A journey to Crete 8

In search of a legend 10

The excavations 12

Former glories 15

Knossos 16

Griffins and lilies 19

Cretans at work 20

Colonists and traders 22

The shipbuilders 24

The quest for metals 26

The foundry 28

The bull leapers 30

A Cretan home 32

Harvests and hunting 34

The mystery of the letters 36

Minoan treasures 38

Santorini 40

The giant wave 42

Devastation 44

The forgotten island 46

Map 6

Kithira (Cythera)

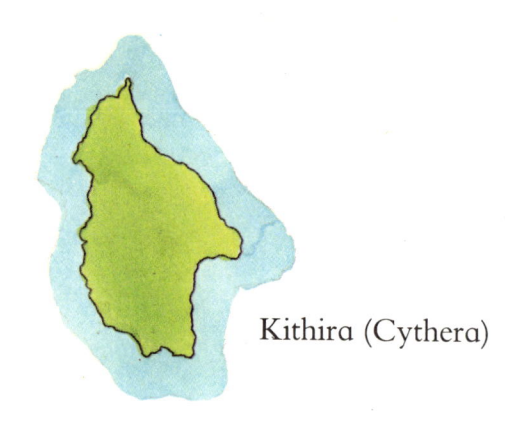

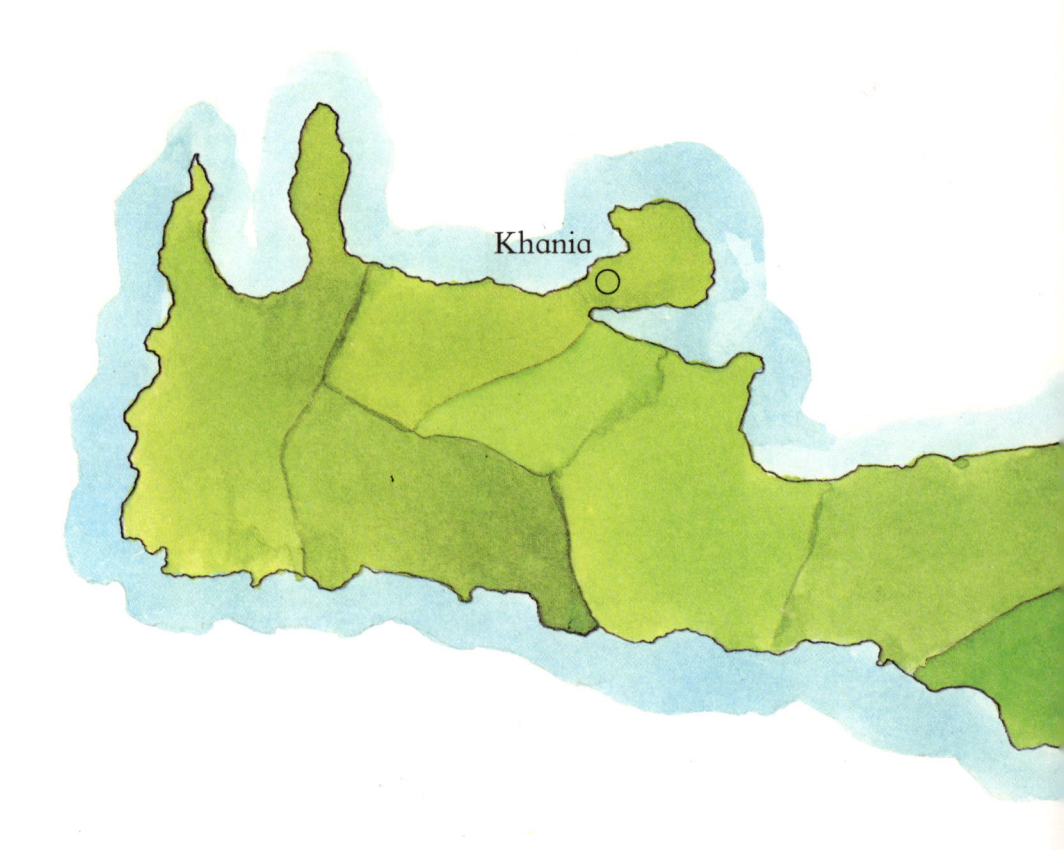

Khania

Mediterranean Sea

Thira (Santorini)

Sea of Crete

CRETE

Iraklion (Candia)
Knossos
Mallia
Monastiraki
Zakros
Ayia Triadha
Gortyn
Gournia
Phaistos

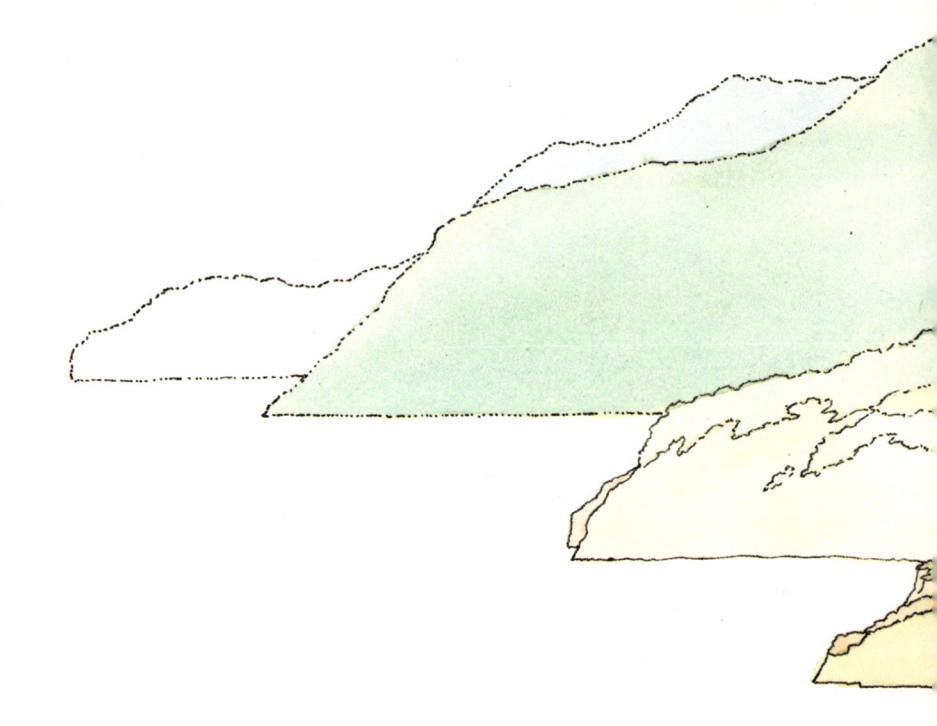

A journey to Crete

You can sail to the island of Crete by ferry. You board your ship in the busy port of Piraeus, which is on the outskirts of Athens, the capital of Greece. Soon the ship is sailing south across the dark blue sea. The smoke and bustle of the city are left far behind.

You pass little islands, baked brown in the summertime by the heat of the sun. Dolphins leap playfully from the swelling waves. At last you can see mountains in the distance: you are approaching Crete, largest of the Greek islands.

But 4,000 years ago the journey took much longer. The sailors would be drenched by spray as their wooden sailing boats plowed through the heavy seas. As they neared the island, they would see a land of forests looming on the horizon. Today's traveler sees a cultivated landscape: groves of orange and lemon trees.

The island of Crete is still beautiful. Arising from its plains are ranges of mountains. The tallest peak is Ida, 8,100 feet high. In winter it is capped with snow.

Crete lies between three continents: Europe is to the north, Asia to the east, and Africa to the south. It is easy to see why this island in the Mediterranean Sea was settled in ancient times, and why it became prosperous. For over 1,500 years, from about 3000 to 1450 BC, Crete was the center of a powerful empire. Its rulers seem to have been known by the title "Minos." From about 2000 BC they governed Crete from the splendid palace of Knossos.

In about 1,450 BC this "Minoan" civilization came to a sudden end. A volcano erupted on the nearby island of Santorini (known in Greek as Thira). A giant tidal wave swamped the Cretan coast and ash rained down on the island, burying the fertile ground.

The magnificent world of Knossos was soon forgotten – except in stories and half-remembered legends.

In search of a legend

In the last century – some 3,300 years after the destruction of Minoan civilization – people began to take an interest in archaeology. The ruins of the ancient Roman city of Pompeii were being uncovered, having been buried under volcanic ash for 17 centuries. In 1870 the German archaeologist Heinrich Schliemann started to excavate the ancient city of Troy.

Heinrich Schliemann was an amateur, a successful businessman who was fascinated by the ancient world. He had read the works of Homer, a Greek poet who probably lived in the 9th century BC. In Schliemann's day nobody believed that Homer's tales were really true. Schliemann's excavation of Troy made them think again. And in 1876 he discovered the ancient city of Mycenae.

In 1886, Schliemann came to Crete. In Homer's poetry there were clear references to an ancient civilization on the island. Indeed, the poet mentioned that at one time there had been 90 towns on Crete. Could it be that this too would be the site of a major discovery?

Heinrich Schliemann reread the myths and legends of ancient Greece. One in particular interested him – the story of the Minotaur. The tale went like this...

A man called Minos was to become King of Crete. He was sent a bull by the sea-god Poseidon. Minos was meant to sacrifice the bull to Poseidon, but he failed to do so.

In a rage, Poseidon made Pasiphae, the wife of Minos, fall in love with the bull. She gave birth – not to a son, but to a terrible monster, the Minotaur. It had the body of a man and the head of a bull.

Daedalus, a famous inventor, built a maze called the Labyrinth under the palace at Knossos. No one who entered the maze could find the way out again. Here the monster was trapped, wandering through the dark passages.

Every year King Minos demanded a tribute from Athens, a city which had been conquered by the Cretans. The tribute took the form of seven boys and seven girls who were devoured by the terrible Minotaur.

One year an Athenian prince, Theseus, joined the children who were to be sacrificed. In Crete he met Ariadne, the daughter of King Minos, and fell in love with her. Ariadne gave Theseus a ball of thread, which he unreeled as he advanced into the Labyrinth. Here he managed to slay the monster. Following the thread back again, he found his way out of the maze. Athens no longer had to pay its horrible tribute.

It can easily be seen how such a legend might have started. The bull was a sacred animal in ancient Crete. It was believed to be a form of the priest-king, the Minos. He was married to the high-priestess of the mother-goddess. The Cretans certainly conquered many Greek cities, and demanded tributes and taxes from them. This story seems to celebrate the end of Cretan rule.

Heinrich Schliemann decided to follow up the story. He offered to buy the land around the Knossos site. Now Heinrich Schliemann was a businessman, and he soon started to haggle over the deal. The plot was meant to include 2,500 olive trees. Schliemann counted them. He could only find 889 trees! He was so angry he left the island.

Four years later Schliemann was dead. However local people digging around the Knossos site unearthed vases and various ancient treasures. These aroused the interest of the great archaeologist – Sir Arthur Evans.

The excavations

Sir Arthur Evans was born in England in 1851. His father was a paper manufacturer with a great interest in science, history and archaeology. Arthur grew up to share his father's interests. He studied at Oxford University and at Göttingen in Germany. In 1884 he became Keeper of the Ashmolean Museum in Oxford.

In 1900 Sir Arthur Evans began to excavate the site at Knossos. As the soil and rubble were carefully cleared away, he could hardly believe his eyes. Knossos was far, far bigger than the palace that Schliemann had excavated at Mycenae. It was a splendid building.

As the excavation continued, it also became clear that Knossos was much *older* than anyone had guessed. Evans now realized that Minoan civilization must have grown up about 3000 BC, and reached its height a thousand years later, when Knossos was built. The palace therefore predated the Trojan War by several hundred years.

Excavations showed that a violent earthquake had shaken the island in about 1700 BC. It was, however, the eruption of a volcano on nearby Santorini that had finally ended Cretan power in about 1450 BC.

Sir Arthur Evans was a patient, likeable man. He supervised the dig at Knossos until 1926 – and the work was far from finished even then. He returned to Oxford and led a busy life. In 1931 he paid another visit to Crete, and finally died in Britain in 1941, at the grand old age of 90.

Other archaeologists had also come to Crete in the early years of this century: the Americans Harriet Boyd and Richard Seager, the Italian Federigo Halbherr. Their work was continued by other scholars up to the present day.

A large number of other sites were excavated along the Cretan coast: Phaistos, Ayia Triadha, Mallia, Zakros and Gournia. Palaces, houses and the remains of towns were unearthed. Yet again, it had been proved that the poetry of Homer was something more than a fantastic tale.

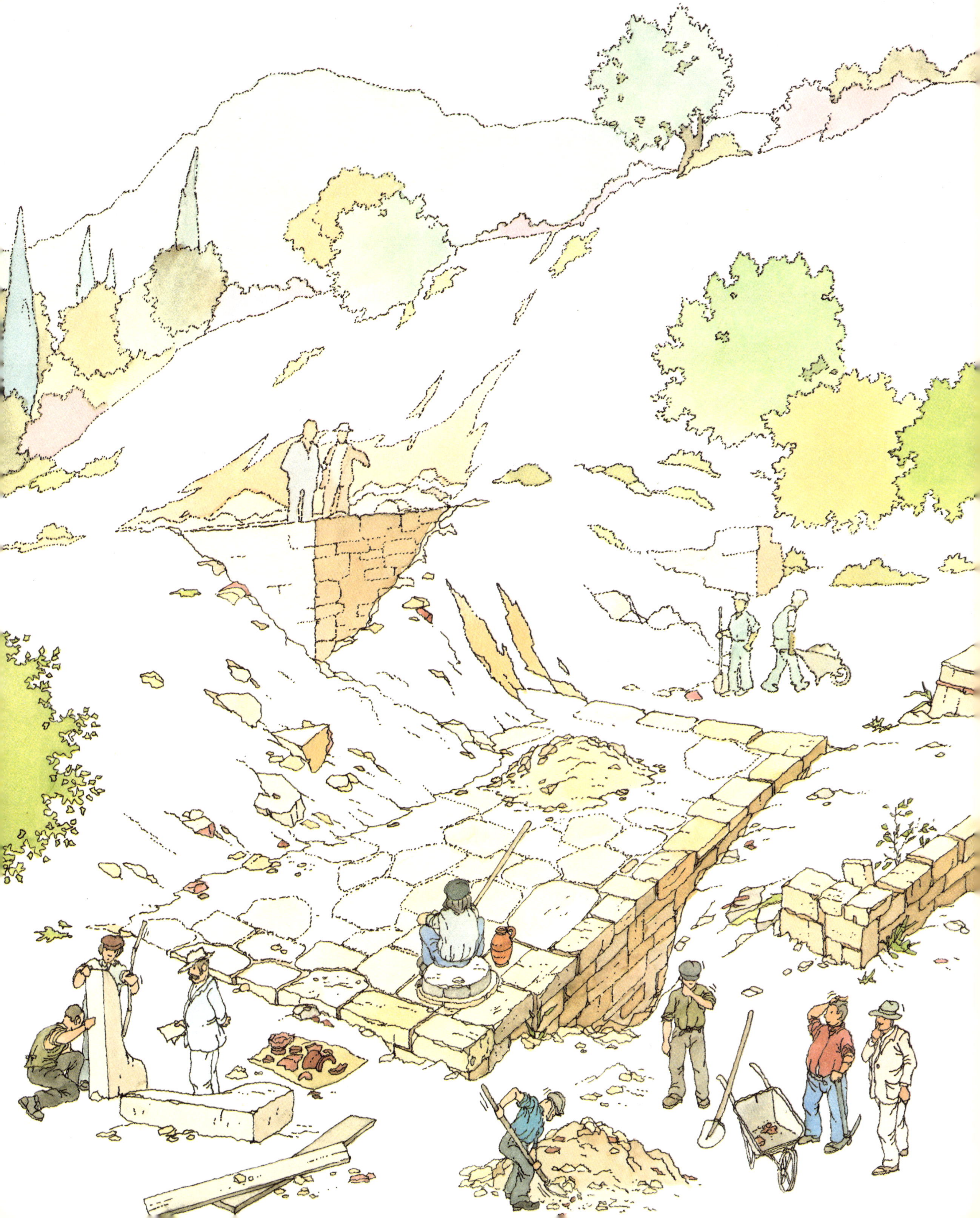

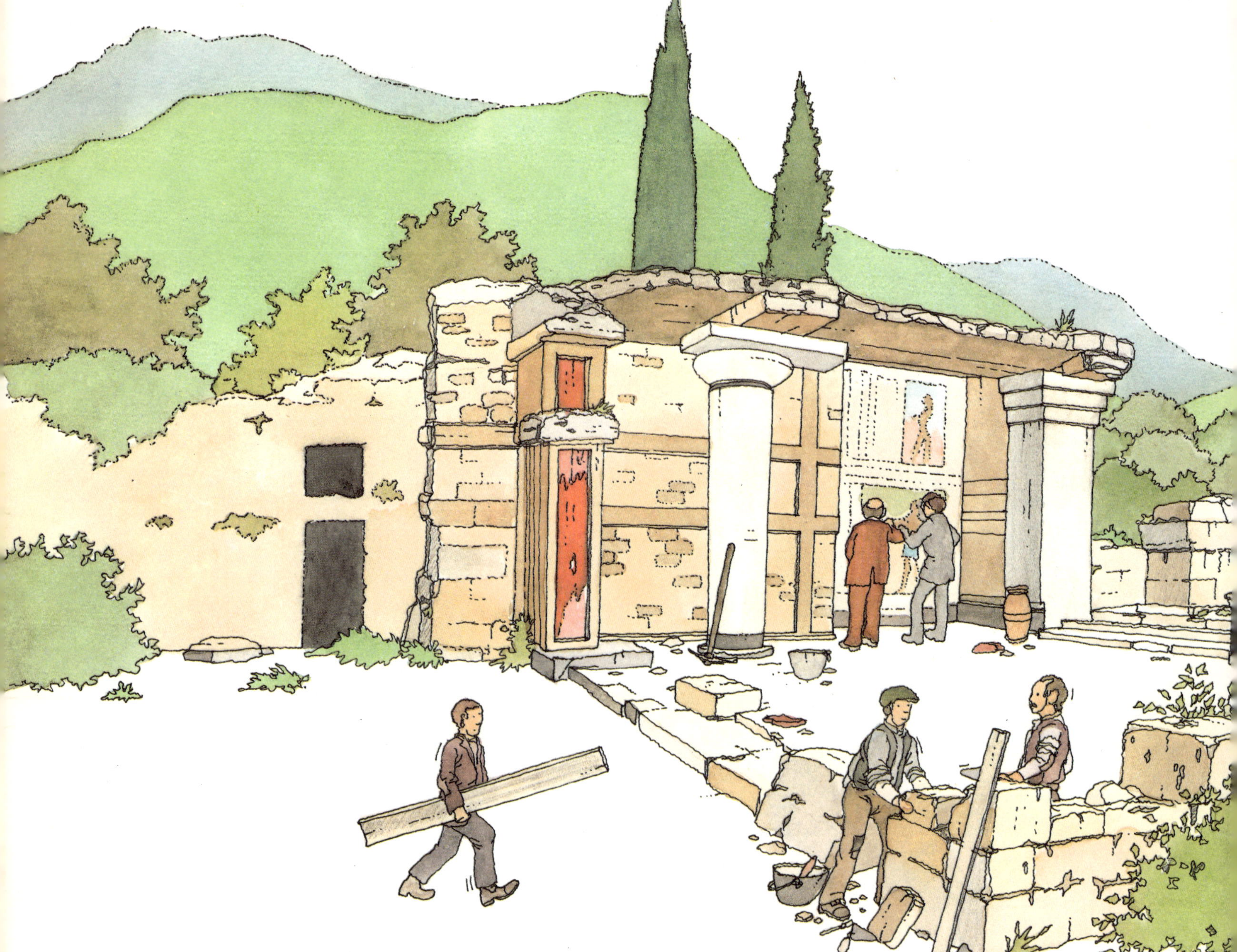

Former glories

Sir Arthur Evans had faced one problem common to many archaeologists. Should he leave everything exactly as he found it, or should he try to restore the building and paintings of Knossos to their former glory?

The excavation had revealed walls of clay. The roofs had been supported by wooden columns painted in bright colors. Frescoes (paintings on plaster) covered the walls of the courtier's rooms. Only a few fragments had survived.

Other rooms included storerooms, wine cellars, water cisterns and kitchens. Outside the palace walls, roads, arenas and market places were now seen.

Sir Arthur Evans decided to restore at least part of the palace. Columns were reconstructed and painted, walls were decorated with frescoes, and pavements were laid. These may still be seen if you visit Knossos today.

Many people have disagreed with Evans' decision. They feel that it would have been better to leave things as they were. Perhaps Evans was too imaginative. We cannot know how the palace *really* looked.

Be that as it may, Crete is still a fascinating place for the visitor. In recent years further archaeological discoveries have been made by accident, during the building of new hotels and roads. We can now understand a great deal more about life in Crete some 4,000 years ago.

Knossos

The palace at Knossos was the center of the powerful Cretan empire, the home of the Minos, or ruler.

The Minos and his court lived in the eastern part of the palace, which was airy and open to the sun. The western part was more enclosed. Here were the sacred places, and cool storerooms also.

The palace had huge doorways and flights of stairs. It was a massive structure – but it did have galleries, balconies and open skylights which made the building seem light and elegant.

Noble families lived in fine houses next to the palace. Here too there were theatres, temples and arenas. Knossos was as crowded and noisy as any town.

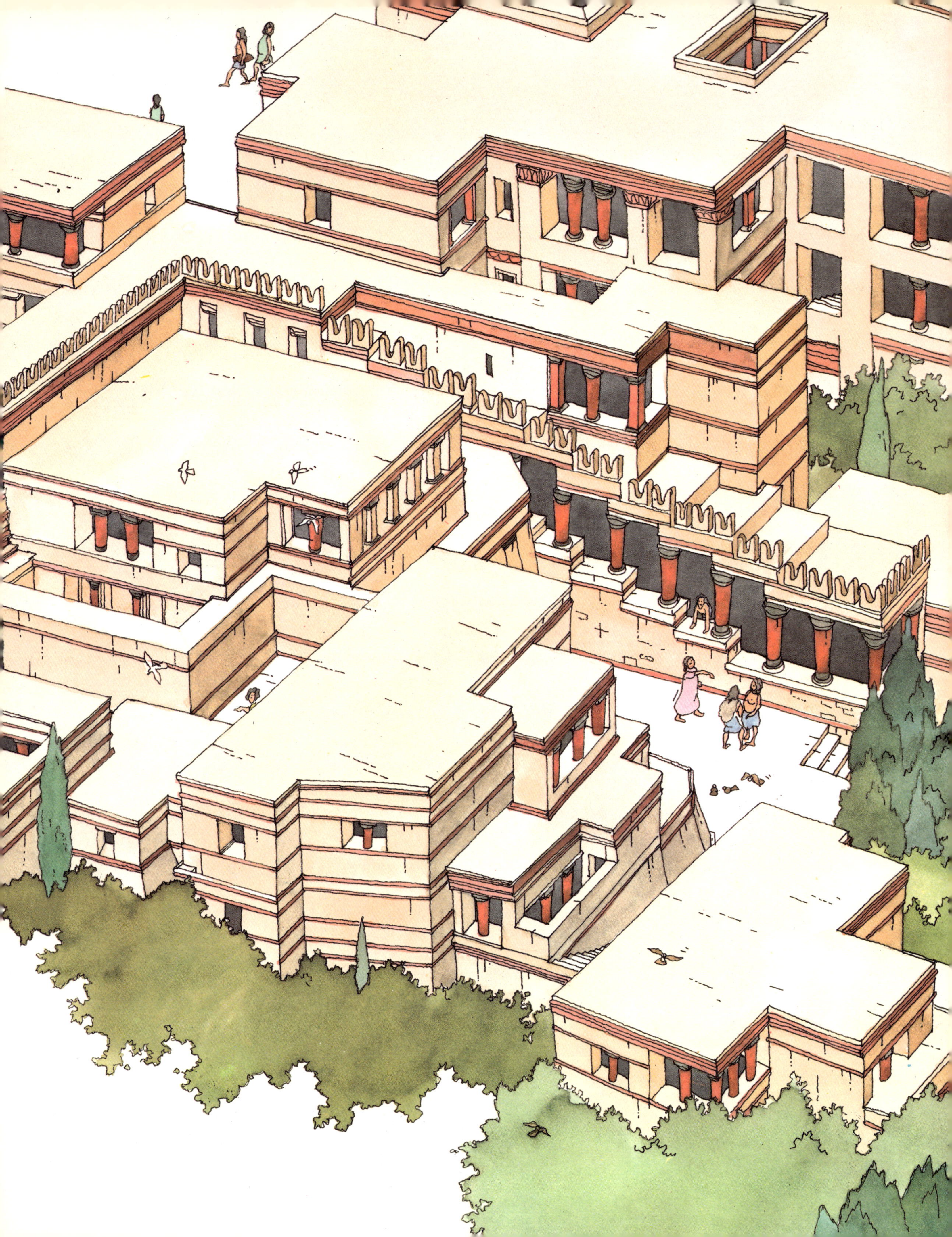

throne room

living room

Griffins and lilies

If you enter the throne room at Knossos it is not hard to imagine it as it was thousands of years ago. The Minos sat in Majesty on a throne of alabaster. Like the pharaohs of ancient Egypt, he was believed to be ruler, high-priest and god on earth. In his hands he held a sceptre and a *labrys* – a double-headed axe which had a special religious meaning.

On the wall behind the throne was a beautiful fresco, a painting of griffins and lilies. Griffins did not really exist of course. They were sacred, mythical creatures. They were shown with the head of an eagle (a symbol of religious power), and the body of a lion (a symbol of worldly power). The griffin's tail was a symbol of the power of the dead over the world of the living.

The Minos was one of the most powerful rulers of the ancient world and his palace was of dazzling splendor. Walls were decorated with many fabulous paintings. The columns supporting the roof in the picture above were painted deep red. They were made of whole tree trunks, turned upside down so that the widest part supported the "capital" – the heading of the column.

painting
frescoes

Cretans at work

When Sir Arthur Evans excavated the palace at Knossos, he made a special point of restoring the splendid paintings which decorated the walls. We know that the Cretans were very skilled at both arts and crafts.

Frescoes were made by painting the walls when the plaster was still damp. Sometimes the frescoes were made "in relief" – the subjects were raised above their backgrounds by building up layer upon layer of plaster before painting.

Some of the paintings were of religious and mythical subjects. Others showed scenes from life at court. Some showed landscapes and seascapes, pictures of flowers, or hunting scenes and animals.

Minoan painters liked to use special colors, which they thought would bring good luck. They used a particular shade of red and a brilliant sky blue. As in ancient Egypt, men were shown in paintings with red bodies, and women with white bodies. Human figures and animals were always shown from a side view. It is from the frescoes that we have learned so many fascinating details of life at Knossos.

The crafts of Minoan civilization were of the same high standard as the paintings. There were jewelers at Knossos, and carvers of ivory from Africa. There were leatherworkers and tanners who dressed skins of wild boar, deer and sheep.

Cretan women were skilled textile workers. They would comb out wool and spin it into yarn. This would then be woven into cloth on a simple weighted loom, and dyed. Women also made vases for storage.

The royal household employed many servants and cooks. Food was stored in large tightly-sealed jars. Wheat, oats, beans, olives, wine and oil were all kept in this way in a cool, dark place – safe from rats and thieving humans. Some foods were kept in underground vats, sealed by a heavy stone slab.

We do not know whether this army of workers were free laborers or whether they were slaves. What is clear is that they were under strict orders from the court, and answerable to the Minos.

storing food

Colonists and traders

The Greek historian Thucydides lived in the 5th century BC, many long years after the end of Cretan power. However, even he mentions the Minoan empire. He tells us that a certain "King Minos" of Crete once built a large fleet and colonized many of the Greek islands, including the Cyclades group, to the north of Crete. Thucydides says that the Cretans cleared the islands of pirates, so that trade could be carried out peacefully.

Thanks to archaeology, we know that Thucydides was telling the truth. Traces of Minoan civilization have been found in nearly all the islands of the Cyclades group: pottery, loom weights used in weaving, daggers, gold cups and many other treasures.

The Cretans had colonies on Milos, Sifnos, Kithira (Cythera) Thira (Santorini), and Kea (Keos). There were also Cretan settlements on the Greek mainland – at Myceanae, for example – on islands such as Rhodes, and in Asia Minor (modern Turkey).

Cretan power spread even farther. Colonists settled on Sicily and in southern Italy. Cretan ships sailed to Spain and even to the British Isles. It seems probable that Minoan trade and civilization influenced a very large part of Europe.

In their dealings, Cretan traders used solid gold weights, in the form of a bull's head. These would be weighed against the gold to be traded or exchanged as money. They have been found far afield, which suggests to us that the Cretan traders were rich and powerful. Their gold was acceptable to everyone.

22

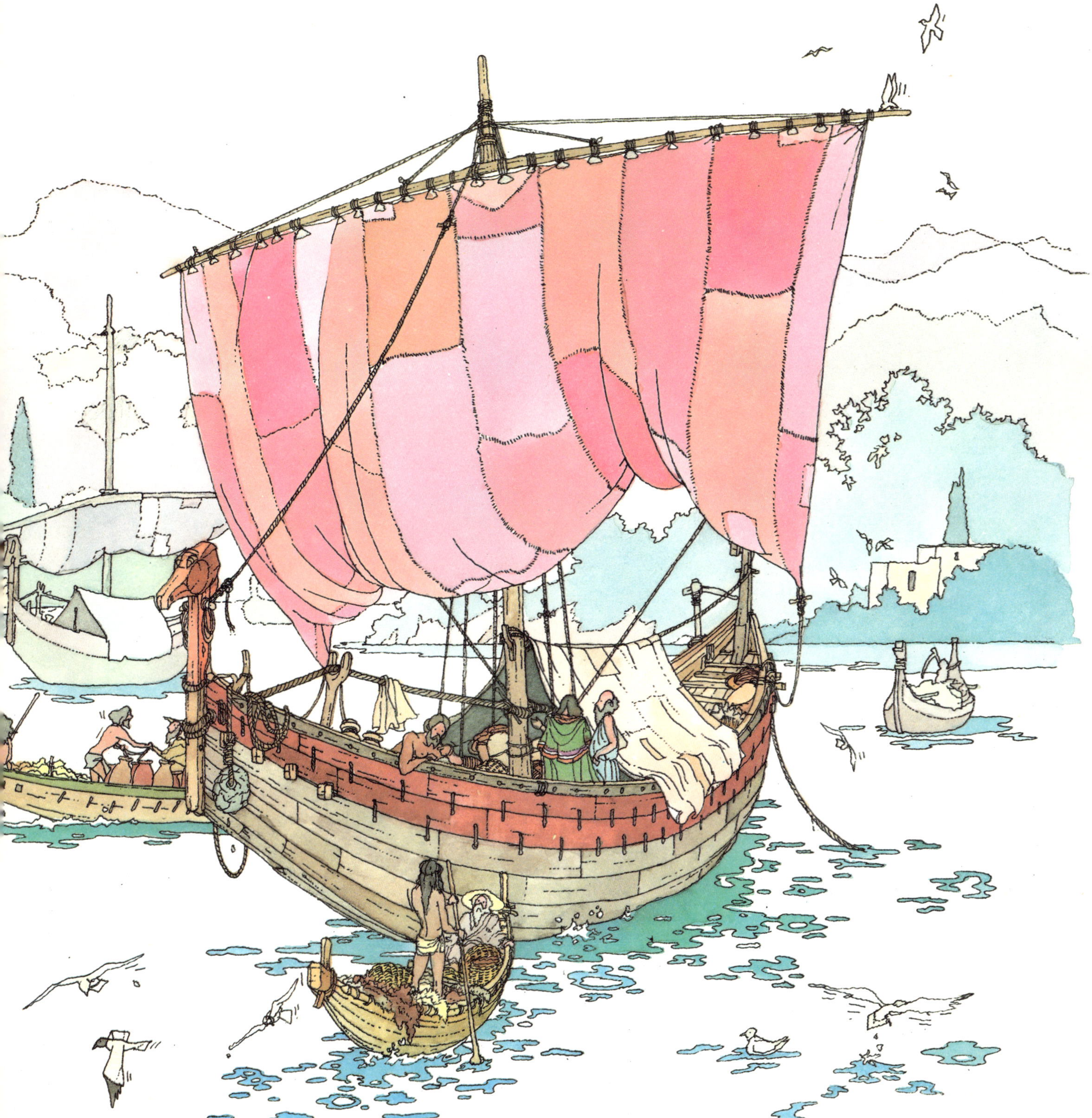

The shipbuilders

Sailing is a dangerous occupation. Early peoples were not always very willing to take to the open sea. The peoples of the eastern Mediterranean region were no exception. Whenever possible they preferred to stay on dry land than to risk their lives in small boats.

Over the ages, however, the peoples of the Greek islands did become experienced and skillful sailors. They traded, settled other lands, and made war. The wealth of Crete, and of later empires in the region, depended on seafaring.

On this page you can see a shipyard near one of the many towns on the coast of Crete. The forests provided timber, and keels were carefully laid down. Hulls and decks were added by skilled carpenters. As Cretan seafarers traveled further afield, their ships became stronger and more seaworthy.

The real test for Cretan ships came when they passed through the Strait of Gibraltar and left the peaceful waters of the Mediterranean. For the high seas of the Atlantic Ocean and the terrible storms of the Bay of Biscay, the Cretans needed sturdy vessels.

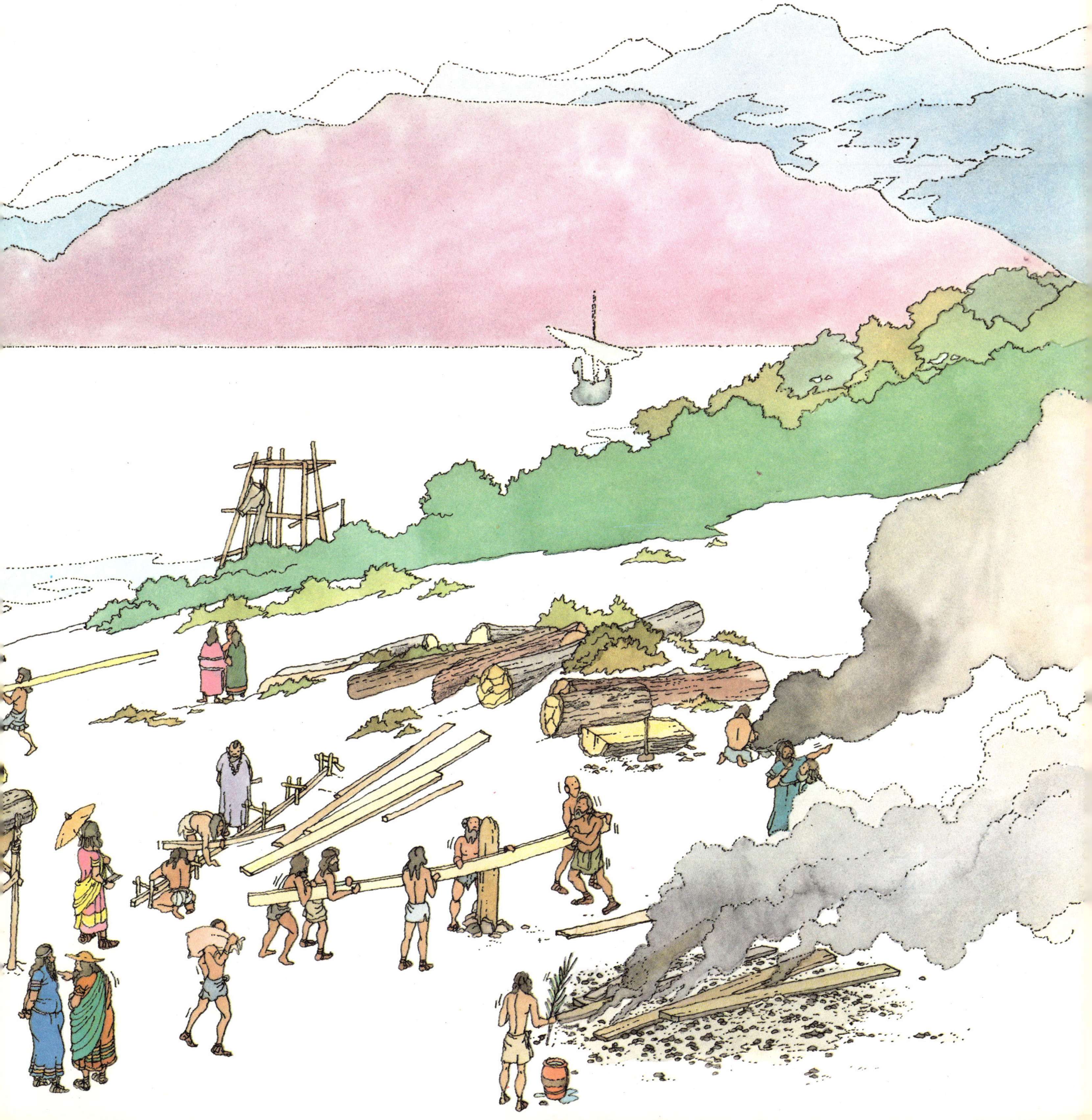

The quest for metals

Why on earth did the Cretans leave the blue seas of the Mediterranean for cold northern waters? The British Isles seemed to be on the edge of the world: distant, misty lands. What could its people, with their primitive settlements and crude stone weapons, offer the Cretans?

They had one very precious commodity: tin. The very first tin mines were in England and in Spain. Tin was valuable because it could be mixed with copper to make bronze.

Bronze was the metal of kings, and the secret of Cretan power. It gleamed like gold, and it was easy to smelt and work. Above all, it was hard, making fine swords and spears.

4,000 years ago, bronze was a new invention. In different parts of the world, from Europe to the valley of the Indus River, people were trying to make copper harder by mixing it with other metals. Just who invented the successful alloy is unknown. However, it was the Cretans who made the dangerous journey westwards to obtain tin to make bronze.

Iron, of course, was not yet used in Europe for weapons or tools. Small amounts of naturally occurring iron were used for ornaments and jewelry, but the metal of the day was bronze. Possession of bronze meant wealth and power. Cretans had bronze in plenty, and with it their influence spread around the known world.

The foundry

These days we often take the metals we use for granted. It is hard for us to imagine just how important bronze was to our ancestors. Instead of clumsy flint axes people now had sharp axes of bronze. Instead of necklaces made of shells they had gleaming bronze jewelry. To them, bronze was more important than gold. It is not surprising that historians sometimes call this period the Bronze Age.

New horizons opened up as people thought up new technical inventions and new forms of artistic expression. Bronze goods were traded far and wide.

The Cretans were expert foundry workers. Tin and copper ore were melted in the furnaces and the molten alloy tipped into molds to harden. Swords and spears were made in this way, as were axes, helmets, shields, bracelets, rings, necklaces and earrings.

From foundries such as the one shown here, bronze goods were sold to Cretans or shipped overseas for trading. The seafarers spread the influence of Minoan civilization far and wide, and the rulers of the island of Crete became wealthy and powerful.

The bull leapers

The Cretans seem to have been a colorful, pleasure-loving people. They are particularly remembered for one of their favorite sports. It was very dangerous, but exciting to watch.

A bull, the sacred animal of Crete, was released into the ring. Young acrobats would vault and spring over the bull's back as it charged, narrowly avoiding the sharp points of the horns.

Perhaps the modern bullfights of Spain have come from a sport such as this. In ancient Crete the contest was fairer – those who took part were unarmed, and the bull was not killed.

Bull leaping was a subject shown on decorated vases and in the wall paintings of Knossos. It is also mentioned in the writings of the Greek philosopher Plato, who was born in the 5th century BC, long after the collapse of Minoan civilization.

Plato says that bull-leaping was a sport on Atlantis, a great island that had once existed in the Atlantic Ocean. Did Atlantis really exist, or was it merely a legend?

Some people believe that there was such a place. Plato also said that there was a land on the far side of the Atlantic, and we now know that he was correct!

Some people have suggested that when Plato wrote of Atlantis, he was talking about the destruction of Crete at the end of the Minoan age. This is unlikely: he clearly knew the difference between the Mediterranean and the Atlantic Ocean.

It seems more likely that in telling of the Atlantis legend, Plato was adding to it memories of another world – the pleasure-seeking court of the Minos.

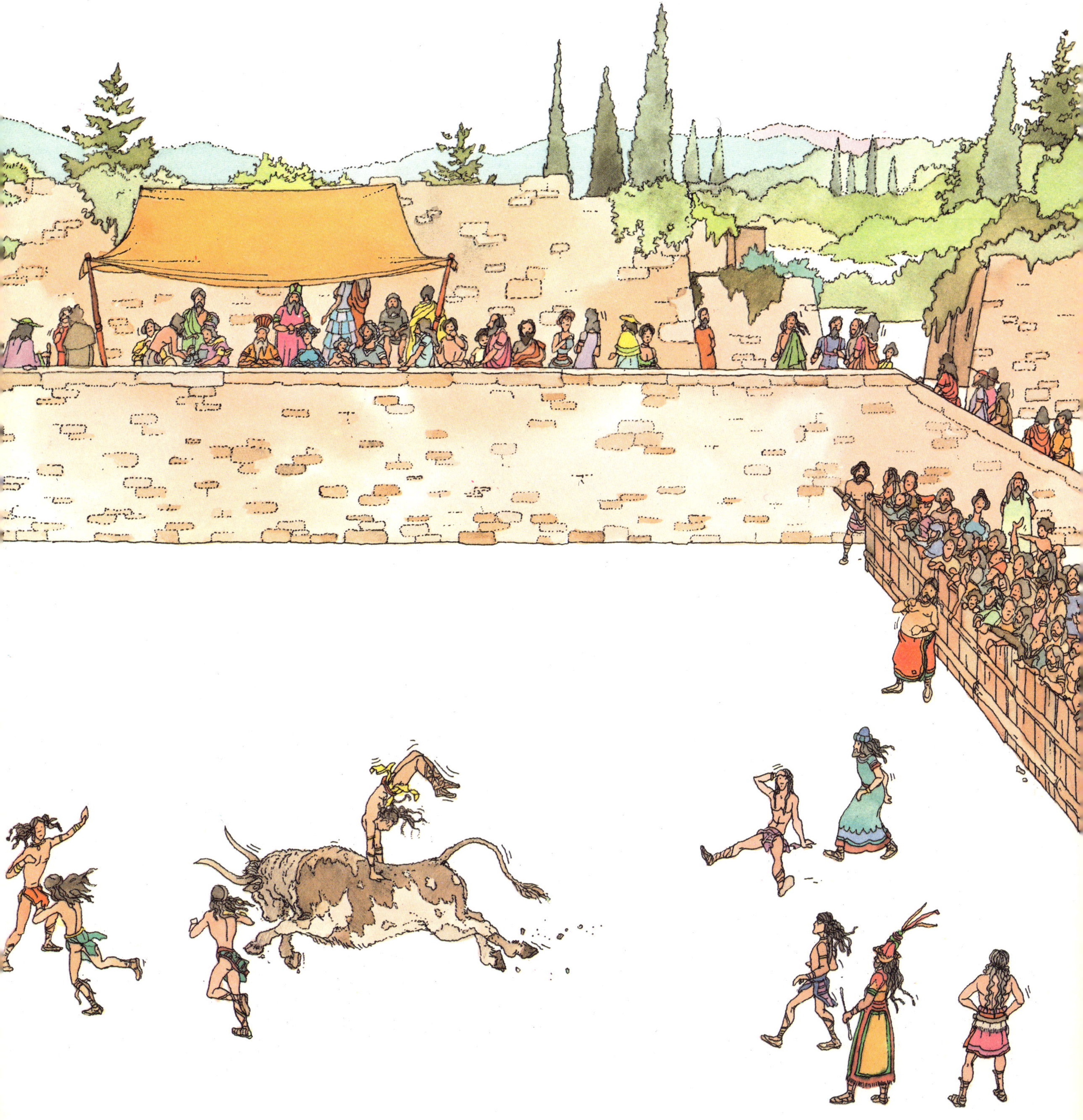

A Cretan home

Kings and queens are not the only people to make history. How did the ordinary Cretans live, away from the royal court? A normal house of the Minoan period probably looked like this.

The walls were rather rough and ready, made of mud bricks supported by a timber framework. The roof was thatched with reeds, and was sometimes covered with a lime cement. The floor might have been of beaten earth, or it might have been paved or cobbled.

The rooms led off from a central courtyard. As in the palace at Knossos, open skylights in the roof kept the rooms light and airy. Rain coming through the opening was collected for household use.

The climate of Crete is typical of the Mediterranean region, being very hot and dry in the summer. Simple houses built on this pattern were used in Mediterranean countries for thousands of years.

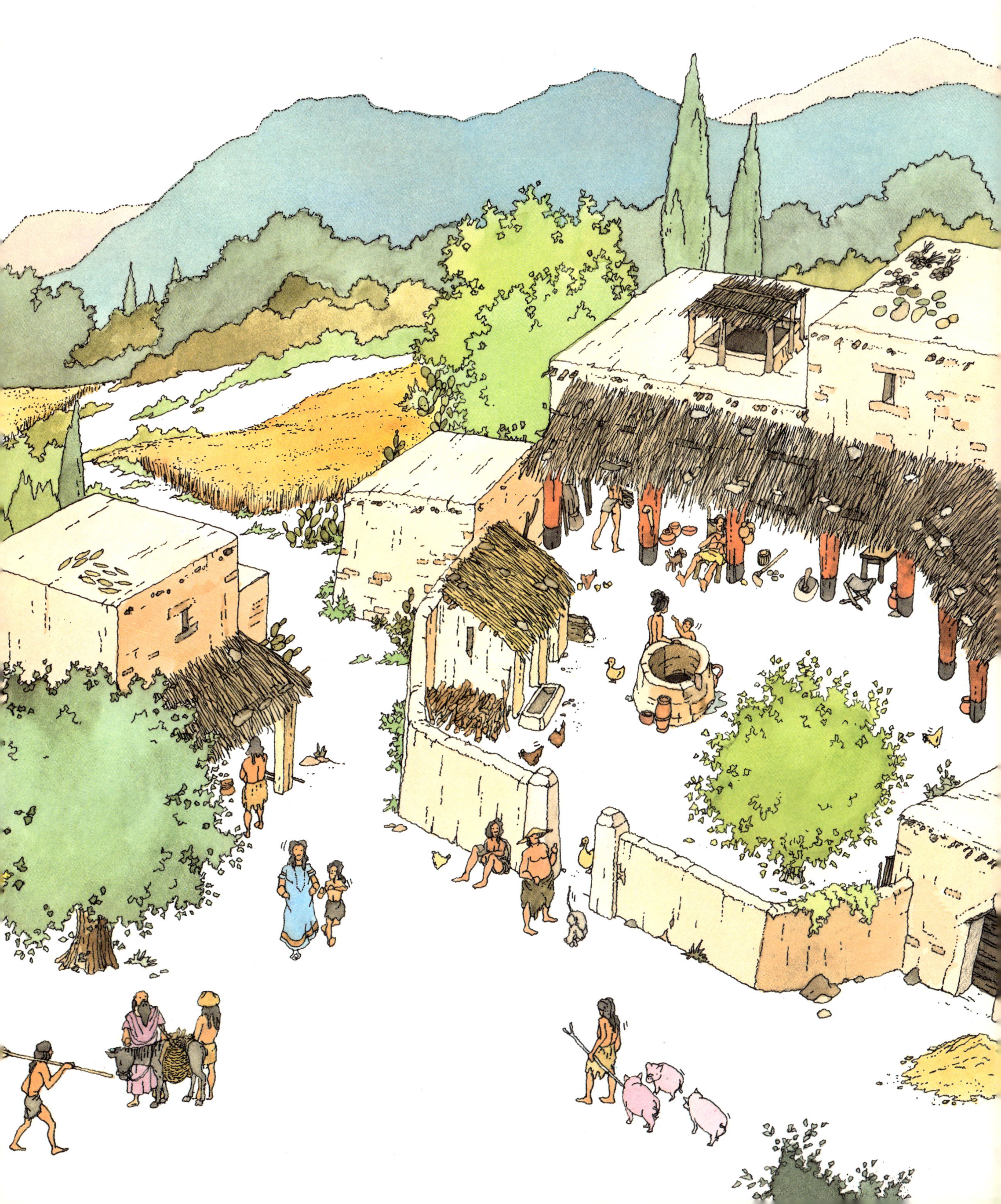

olive grove

Harvests and hunting

We know quite a lot about everyday life in ancient Crete. Archaeologists have found many important clues – vases, paintings, decorated pottery and metal objects. Unfortunately wood, cloth and leather did not survive (which they did in ancient Egypt, thanks to the dry desert sand). What do these clues tell us? How did the ancient Cretans farm, and what did they eat.

Today the Cretans grow all kinds of fruit, including bananas. 4,000 years ago the most important crops were wheat, millet and barley, from which they made a simple kind of beer. Bronze hatchets were used to clear the forests for sowing and to provide timber. The soil was tilled with a simple wooden plow.

As in all Mediterranean countries, grapes and olives played a very important part in the diet. Some people say that vines and olive trees were first cultivated on this island.

The olive tree was sacred to the Minoan Cretans. In the autumn the country people would beat the branches of the trees until the olives fell to the ground. They were steeped in hot water and then pressed into a pulp. Out of the olive pulp ran a clear golden-green liquid – olive oil.

Both black grapes and white grapes were grown and were made into a very good wine. Cretan red wine was well known in ancient times. Every autumn grapes would be laid out and dried under the sun to make raisins, to be eaten during the winter months.

The Cretans kept all kinds of farmyard animals: chickens, sheep, pigs and cattle. Beehives provided honey, the only thing they had to sweeten food.

Fishermen used lines and nets to bring in their catch, and wicker baskets like today's lobster pots. Like the modern Greeks, the ancient Cretans were very fond of eating octopus. These would be speared along rocky shores, landed and killed.

Hunting was another important source of food. Today the only large wild animal to be found on Crete is a species of long-horned goat. However in ancient times the island was teeming with deer and wild boar. Lions were released from captivity and hunted

For most Cretans, however, life was spent tilling the soil and gathering in the harvest. For thousands of years this way of life continued without change.

vineyard

The mystery of the letters

One of the hardest problems facing the archaeologist is how to understand ancient forms of writing. When a mysterious new script is discovered, it is often impossible to work out what it means unless it is accompanied by another piece of writing in a language we understand.

This was the case with the picture-writing (or hieroglyphics) of the ancient Egyptians. A stone was found near Rosetta which had an inscription in three languages. By comparing the Egyptian hieroglyphics with the Greek script, it was possible to understand the former.

Unfortunately, no Rosetta stone has been found in Crete to help us understand ancient inscriptions. The earliest Cretan script, like that of the ancient Egyptians, is made up of symbols – fish, stars, hands etc. Its meaning remains a mystery to this day.

Two forms of linear writing seem to have developed from these hieroglyphics. Scholars call the earliest of these "Linear A," and the later script "Linear B". Linear B was in use at the end of the Minoan period, and is the only one which is understood today.

In 1936 Sir Arthur Evans held a conference on Knossos. Michael Ventris, a young British scholar who was present, became fascinated by Linear B. For years he puzzled over the strange writing, which had no less than 87 different symbols. At last in 1952 he had worked out its meaning.

The pieces of writing that had survived were in fact records of accounts for the palace of Knossos. The writing had been scratched on tablets of soft clay. The writer would have used tablets

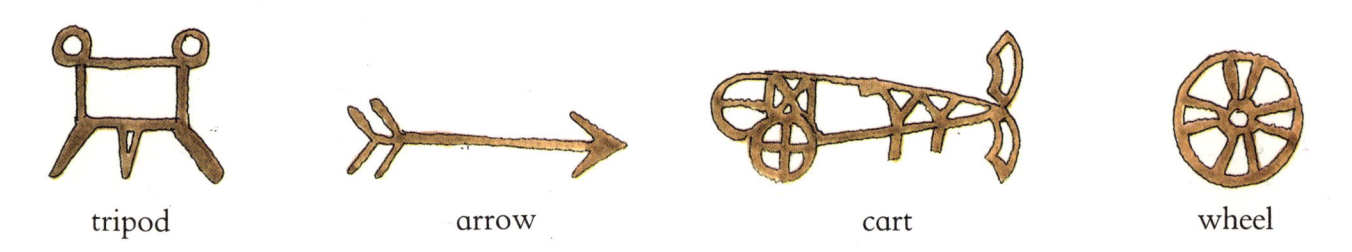

man   woman   horse   pig   cup   sword

tripod   arrow   cart   wheel

the Phaistos disc

like these as a daily tally, making new tablets at the start of each day. The surviving tablets had been baked in a fire, presumably by accident, and so had been hardened and preserved.

One of the greatest mysteries is a piece of picture-writing found at Phaistos. It is a disc of clay six inches across. Symbols have been pressed into the clay with wooden blocks on both sides. Was it originally made in Crete? We do not know. It dates from about 1600 BC and there is nothing else like it. Its spiraling symbols of flowers, running figures and crested heads pose a puzzle we may never solve.

37

stone seals

decorated vase

soapstone bull's head

clay bull

Minoan treasures

The pieces of writing unearthed by the archaeologists on Crete are mostly lists of farm produce or goods in the storerooms of Knossos. However the Cretans were not just simple farmers and merchants. Other treasures that were discovered prove that in the Minoan period they were great lovers of beauty, who enjoyed the very finest things that craft workers of their day could produce.

Among the most famous finds was that of a bull's head made of black soapstone. This would be used to pour out offerings to the gods. Many small religious statues have been found, including some of the snake goddess. Many cups and vases came to light, and

snake goddess

cups of beaten gold

archaeologists date the different stages of Minoan civilization by the way in which they are decorated.

One of the most numerous finds on Crete was of small stone "seals" like the ones shown above left. Some of these were offerings left at the shrine of a god or goddess. Others were personal signets, worn on the finger and used as a sort of signature or authorization.

Perhaps the most common use of these seals was by merchants, as a sort of guarantee or trademark. In ancient times there were of course no airtight glass jars or cans. Goods were stored and transported in pots and jars sealed with clay. The seal would be pressed into the clay, so that it was easy to see if the opening had been tampered with. Every Cretan merchant had his own seal.

Santorini

Across the Sea of Crete, 60 miles to the north, lies the island of Santorini. In Greek it is known as Thira. One of the Cyclades group, Santorini was once a colony of Crete.

Santorini was famous for its beauty in ancient times, and it still is today – even though it has changed shape. Once it was circular. Today it is split into several parts. Between the largest part of the island and the other pieces lies the sea.

A clue as to what happened to Santorini lies in the pumice stone which today streaks its black rocks. Pumice is a rock created by volcanic explosions, and Santorini was indeed once the site of a volcanic peak. It must have been about 5300 feet high.

Sometime around 1500 BC the island was rocked by a series of earthquakes. And then the unimaginable happened. A mighty explosion blew the volcano apart. At the same time part of the island collapsed, forming an underwater crater or "caldera" 1300 feet below the ocean floor.

Ash and stones were flung high into the air and caught by the winds. A vast tidal wave swelled out to sea, and rolled southwards towards Crete.

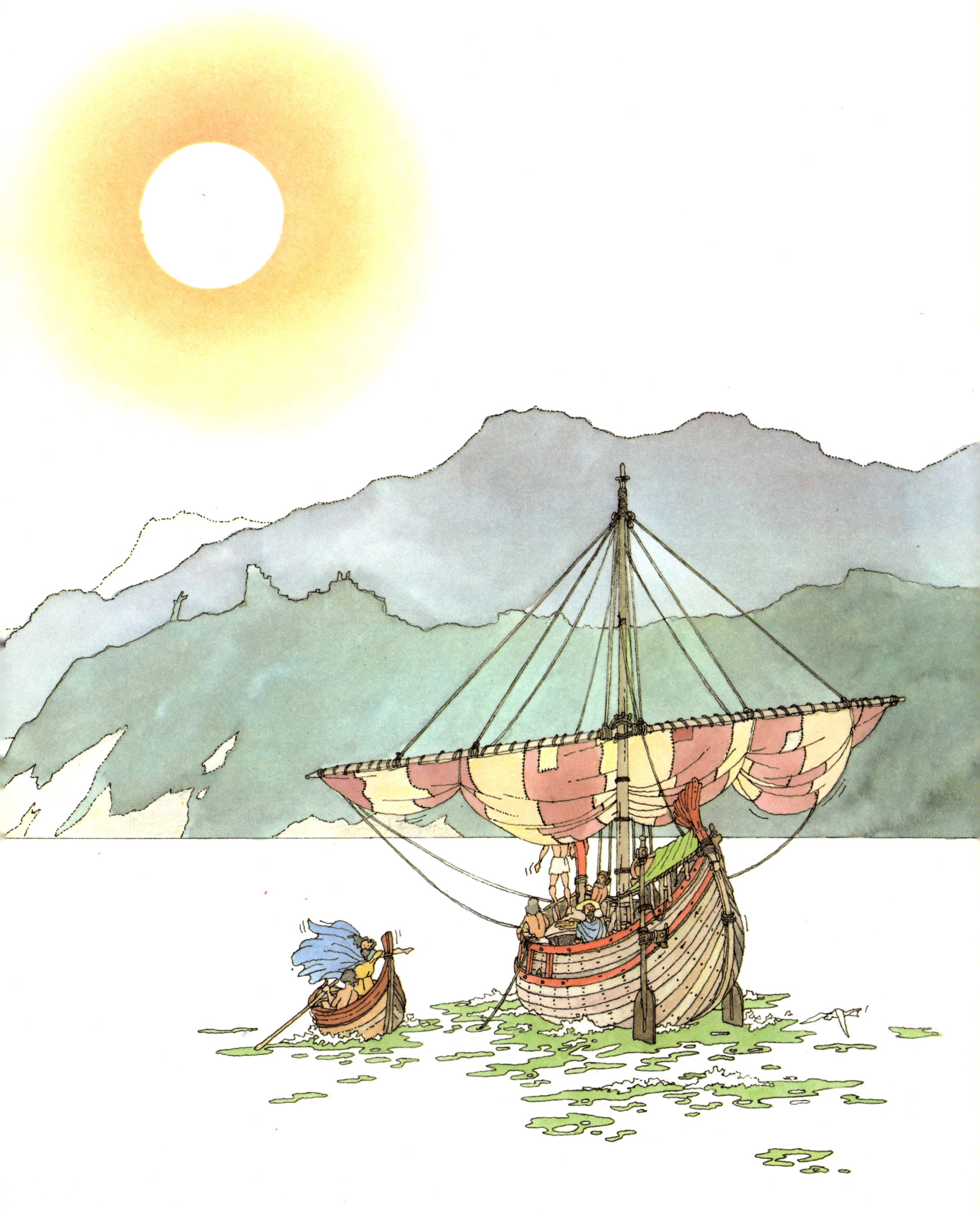

The giant wave

It seemed like the end of the world. Cretan fishermen turned and raced for their home ports – in vain. A tidal wave of terrifying size was rolling towards them. We think it must have been between 100 and 130 feet high.

The wave swept their tiny boats aside and crashed into the northern shores of Crete with a devastating impact. Ships, harbor buildings and palaces were smashed into rubble and sucked back into the sea. Hundreds of thousands of people were drowned.

The worst eruption in modern times was in 1883. A volcano on Krakatoa, an island between Sumatra and Java, erupted with a roar that could be heard nearly 2900 miles away. The Santorini explosion was probably *five times* as powerful as Krakatoa. Within minutes the northern coast of Crete was reduced to a watery wilderness.

Knossos, three miles inland, probably survived the worst of the tidal wave. The middle of the island and the southern coast were spared. But not for long. Another disaster was on its way.

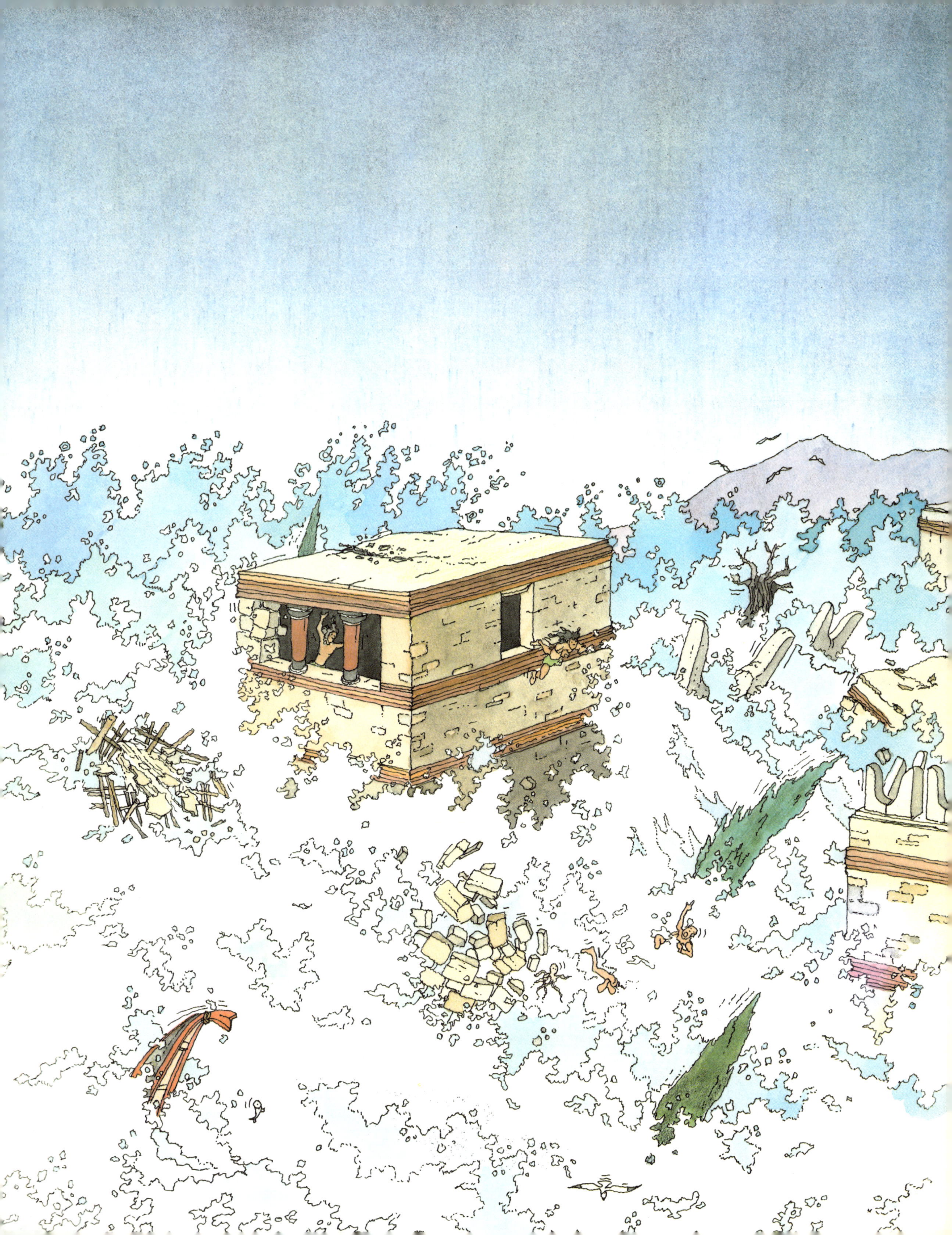

Devastation

As the ocean battered the coast of Crete, the sky grew dark. Winds whipped the ash from Santorini into great black clouds. Rocks and pebbles and dust began to rain down on the island.

Some natural disasters only have a limited effect. An earthquake in 1700 BC had destroyed houses and palaces on Crete – but the survivors had been able to rebuild them. Even the great tidal wave had only destroyed parts of the island. However volcanic ash is far more deadly. It was ash that was to destroy Pompeii, and it was ash that devastated Crete.

It fell like snow, burying towns, palaces, fields and crops. Noblemen, priestesses, merchants and farmers choked and were suffocated. Four inches of volcanic ash on a field can prevent any crops from growing for ten years. On Crete over three feet of ash fell in some places.

The effect of the poisonous chemicals left on the soil seems to have been particularly severe on this occasion. For some 50 years the earth was to be a barren wasteland. A gray desert took the place of the golden fields of wheat, the sunny vineyards and the sacred olive groves.

A solidified layer of volcanic ash has been found as much as 420 miles from Crete. On the island itself the few survivors had nothing left to live for. The great Minoan empire had been destroyed – within a few hours.

The forgotten island

What happened after the terrible disaster? We know very little. Few visitors would have wished to anchor in such a place. Robbers and pirates probably raided the island, looting the ruined palaces and towns. Cretan survivors tried to pick a living from the barren island, or sailed away to other places. Gradually, however, the wind and the rain did their work. The ash broke up or washed away and plants began to grow again.

The power of the Minoan rulers was past. Towns which had been under Cretan rule became free. The Greek mainland had hardly been touched by the eruption, and the Mycenaeans were now able to sail south and take control of the Cretan villages that remained.

The citadel of Mycenae, excavated by Heinrich Schliemann, was built about the time of the destruction of Crete. Mycenaeans led the attack on Troy and became rich and powerful. They were finally defeated by Dorian Greeks, who invaded Crete itself in about 1100 BC.

Never again did Crete know the splendor of the Minoan period. The world of Knossos passed into legend: it seemed like some golden age of the distant past. The rulers of Crete were remembered as one mythical person, King Minos, whose wife's monstrous offspring roamed the Labyrinth.

Memories of Crete seem to have lingered on. Homer wrote that the hero Ulysses visited an island called "Phaeacia," where the inhabitants loved dancing, hot baths and comfortable beds. He describes them as skillful sailors and merchants. And as we have seen, Plato linked Crete with Atlantis, another legendary island that still fascinates us today.

By modern times we had forgotten eveything of Crete's true history. Not until Sir Arthur Evans uncovered the walls of Knossos did we realize the magnificence of the Minoan court. And not until the excavation of Santorini did we discover how it met its end: it was not destroyed by invasion or by civil wars, but by the forces of nature itself.

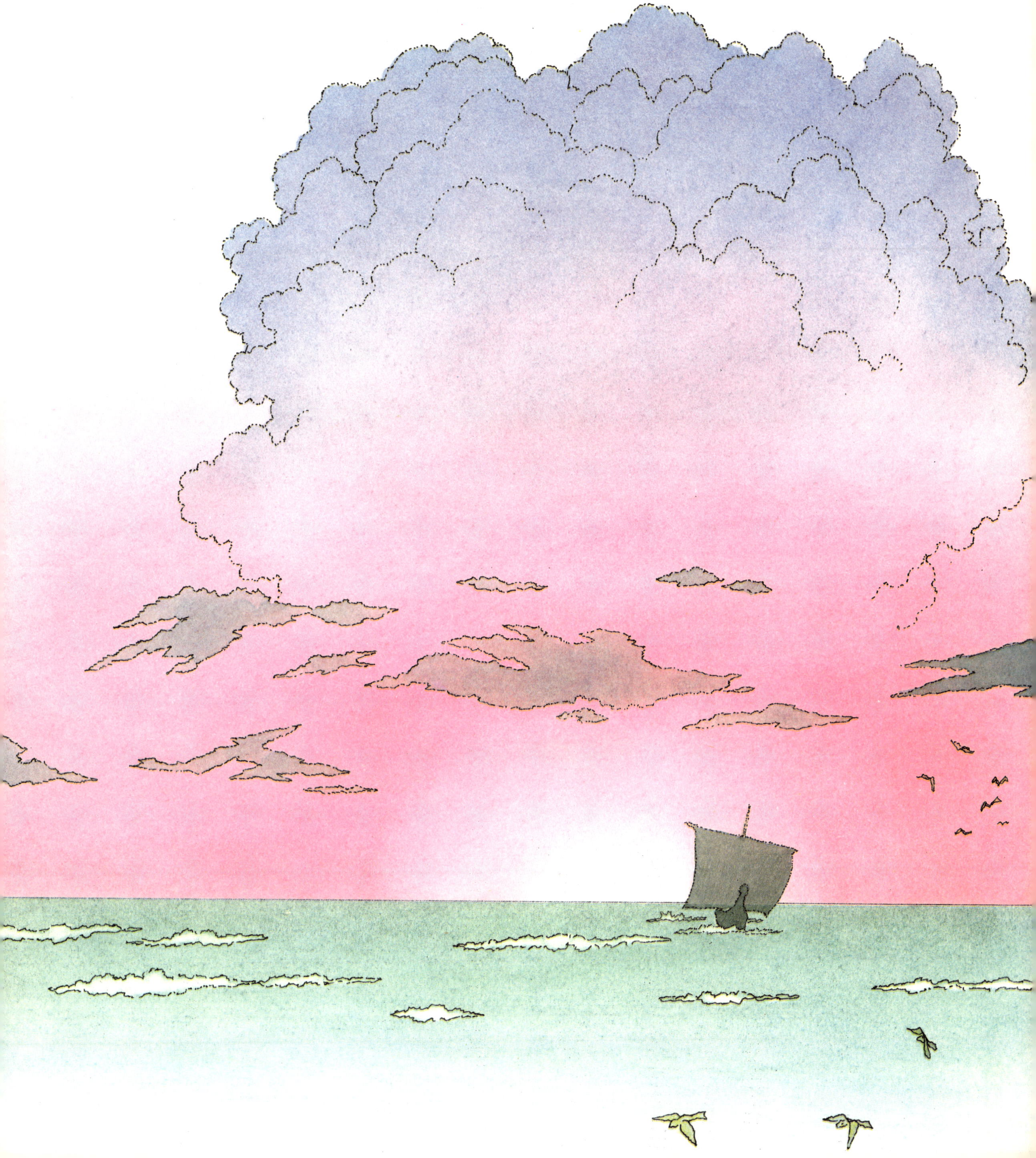